A PRIMER FOR A SELF-MANAGED CONDO HOMEOWNERS' ASSOCIATION

BY

JEWEL PICKERT

ISBN-13: 978-0-692-05897-8 (Conflitel Resolutions, LLC)

Printed in the United States of America

First Printing, 2018

DEDICATION

To Mom and Dad, who instilled in me the work ethic, perseverance, and confidence to tackle whatever I wanted to do in life. Without their loving guidance in my early years and beyond, I wouldn't have been able to become the person (or board member) I am today.

TABLE OF CONTENTS

INTRODUCTION

In 2018, I will have lived in a Minnesota condominium for 30 years. During that time, I have served on and off the board. Presently, I've been a board member for nine years and counting. My title remains vice president and secretary, because our bylaws state one person cannot serve as president and secretary at the same time. No one else wants to be secretary; therefore, I serve a dual role as stated.

Our association of 24 homeowners requires a total of three to five board members. Now we have three. One member is the president and treasurer, while another is a member. We have an accountant do our financials.

Over the years, we have experimented with different property management companies and with self-management. We recently switched from a property management company to being self-managed.

Our property consists of one three-story building with eight units per floor. In addition, there are three garage buildings, with each having eight garages. We have no special amenities, like meeting rooms, pools, or offices. Just an electrical closet under one set of stairs and a plumbing closet under another. A small front vestibule contains our mailboxes and a lockbox with keys that only the fire department has access to in the event of an emergency. We also have a small, fenced-in, concrete slab between two garage sections for our dumpster and recycling bin.

Each condo unit has two bedrooms, one bathroom, a kitchen, and a combination dining room and living room, plus a patio or deck.

Although the guidelines I'll be sharing are for our condo association, they would also apply to self-managed townhome associations.

If your association runs smoothly, you may not benefit from this book, other than to see what happens elsewhere, and, perhaps, to glean a couple of ideas. It has been my experience that more often than not, condo board members and homeowners, and even some property management companies, lack the experience and/or knowledge required to run an association successfully.

No one taught me. I gained my experience through trial and error and persistence. It occurred to me that new board members could benefit from my experience by shortening their learning curve; hence, this book.

You may have even heard of another more compelling reason to master what it takes to run an association efficiently and effectively. If you don't have effective guidelines, someone could take advantage by embezzling money, for instance. Several cases regarding corruption of this nature have appeared in the news. For example, in June, 2017, www.kstp.com and others reported that a former chief financial officer of Durand and Associates, a property management company in S. St. Paul, Minnesota was being investigated for embezzlement. More than 30 condo associations may have been impacted.

Unfortunately, embezzlement cases are far from rare. Community Associations Network has reported on embezzlement cases involving a man in Bergen County, New Jersey; an accountant in Ft. Collins, Colorado; a community manager in Nevada; and a management company employee in Scottsdale, Arizona, to name a few. All cases pertained to homeowners' associations. Even without ill intent, negligence or mistakes could occur simply because of ignorance.

It pays to be informed. Typically, if funds are misallocated, misspent, or stolen, the only way to replenish funds is for the homeowners to pay more, if they can't get it through insurance or a lawsuit. With so much interconnection, everyone has a stake.

What some people fail to realize is that a condo association is a business. Ours is incorporated in the state of Minnesota. Running it properly requires a business mindset. This mindset can be foreign to board members who have never experienced it before.

You might think we're in the condominium business. We're not. We're actually in the people business, whether we're talking about homeowners, vendors, a property management company, or someone else. The main tool we have at our disposal is communication, for without effective and accurate communication, none of our guidelines would work properly.

The guidelines for self-management in this book are meant to show how a business mindset and board commitment can make your condo association run like a well-oiled machine. Some information regarding property management companies is included for those toying with the idea of working with one.

If nothing I've stated so far makes sense to you, don't panic. I'll explain everything in the following pages. The table of contents is detailed enough so that you can use this book as a reference. Chapter 1 will give you a peek at where different people associated with your property are coming from. This is quite helpful when you're dealing with issues or concerns. Unless you know where you're at, it can be difficult to move forward.

You will also see what a basic association structure looks like and how to communicate wisely in Chapters 2 and 3.

Chapters 4 and 5 will show you the guidelines that have worked for us. You can certainly adapt them for your own use.

The appendices offer a glossary, additional articles for your reference, and some sample forms.

My hope is that you will find some worthwhile nugget you can use to help your association be better than it was before.

Jewel Pickert
January, 2018
Minnesota

P. S. Throughout this book, I have mixed the use of the pronouns he and she indiscriminately.

Disclaimer: I am not an attorney or an accountant and cannot give legal or financial advice. Each condo association is different. I only offer information and guidelines that have worked for our condo association.

Chapter 1:

BASIC FOUNDATION

First, let's create a foundation for what the association oversees vs. what a homeowner is responsible for.

Association Concerns vs. Condo Homeowner Concerns

With any association property, typically, there are common elements and limited common elements. Common elements refer to places where everyone can go, like the hallways, stairwells, lobby areas, parking lot, and lawn. Usually, the association pays for any upkeep of the common elements.

Limited common elements refer to items for which the association may or may not have responsibility. It depends. For example, a patio may be considered a limited common element in the bylaws. If a condo owner damages his patio, he could be liable for the repair costs. If water or wind damage a patio, it's possible the association would bear this cost. With limited common elements, the board determines which costs pertain to condo owners vs. the association. Any decisions have to be enforced fairly and consistently for everyone.

In our bylaws, water pipes are limited common elements, even if they're in the walls and not visible to the condo owner. If a pipe leaks, the condo owner of that pipe pays for the repair cost.

Since many times, a water leak affects more than one unit, we handle water pipe leaks this way. A board member calls the plumber and oversees the initial investigation of the leak and arranges for the fix. The board uses association funds to pay the plumber after receiving the plumber's invoice. Then, based on the plumber's findings, the association bills the responsible condo owner for any costs incurred. Depending on the amount, the board may opt to allow the condo owner to pay in installments without interest until the bill has been paid off.

A condo owner, of course, takes care of everything inside his condo and garage.

If a condo owner wants to alter the building by taking out a wall or constructing something that would interfere with the integrity of the condo building, he needs to get approval from the board first. It's likely in this case that his request would be denied.

For a complete list of both common and limited common elements, refer to your governing documents.

A Look at Mindset

Without good communication, an association would not function to the best of its capability. For clarity of purpose, objectives, and execution, it helps to understand the mindset of different players in the condo world to communicate effectively.

Mindset of a Homeowner

For a new, first-time condo owner, the governing documents, the rules for the association, can be a dizzying morass of legal mumbo-jumbo. It can be difficult to find someone who can explain the verbiage in a clear, simple manner. Perhaps board members even disagree on an interpretation of the documents.

Since we all have limited time, we typically choose to spend it on our own priorities. A condo owner may dismiss the governing documents as just so much fine print. It would just be common sense, right? He'll figure it out on his own. Until a board member informs him that he has violated a rule in the bylaws. If the condo owner fails to bone up on those documents, he could find himself violating all sorts of rules and, possibly, having to pay a fine.

And then, the situation turns personal. He wonders why the board is picking on him. All of a sudden, condo living isn't so much fun anymore. Every time he sees a board member, he cringes--or lashes out.

Contrast that mindset with this one. A new condo owner reviews the governing documents and asks questions until he understands how the association works and how he can best fit into the community. He may even attend a board meeting to meet the other board members.

He follows the rules. If he doesn't agree with something, he follows whatever the proper protocol is for that association to get his concern addressed.

He gains confidence with his ability to navigate the system. It's easy for him to stay out of trouble and to contribute in an effective manner. For him, condo living fits his needs well. If your condo owners fit this type, consider yourself fortunate. Treat them like gold.

Mindset of a Board Member

For a first-time condo board member, she may wonder what in the world she got herself into. She might feel overwhelmed with everything she has to learn. The governing documents don't make a lot of sense. Reading them is dry and boring. She doesn't know the history of the property. And just what is she supposed to do, anyway? She may have limited time. She ran to become a board member, because she figured she wouldn't need to do much. After all, how hard could it be?

For a long-time board member, she may be wondering how she can get others to relieve her of some of her workload. Or, she may be lulled into a feeling of complacency, because she likes the status quo. Or, perhaps she relishes having a certain amount of authority or power and would rather dictate than do.

Reality Check

Being a board member is definitely a service position. You represent all homeowners, not just yourself. It's guaranteed there will be a variety of opinions. But, if you think of the association as a group of homeowners who are in this together, you will be more apt to make decisions for the best interests of all.

Do what you need to do to understand the governing documents. It's imperative. There should be a solid reason for every decision you make. If you can't define a solid reason, you don't know the issue well enough to make a decision. After the board has done its due diligence on a matter, stick with the decision, and move on.

Be approachable. People have to feel comfortable telling you about their ideas, opinions, and concerns. To do this well, you have to believe you're helping, not dictating. Sometimes, this is a thankless job. You may resent the time you're spending on board activities, while others busy themselves with their everyday lives.

Just remember, you own a unit as well. By taking care of the property, you ensure your condo is taken care of, too. And, you're developing a skill set, such as planning, organization, conflict resolution, meeting preparation, and effective communication and collaboration skills, which you can market in other areas of your life.

Disagreements will occur. Sometimes, workloads on the board are uneven. Not everyone knows how to train well. Not everyone likes change. Not everyone commits to learning what they need to know to be effective. For ways to handle these as well as other matters, refer to the guidelines sections.

Mindset of a Property Manager

A property manager manages several associations; yet, they may all seem like a blur. Many of the issues and concerns are similar. He forgets what exactly is happening with which homeowner association. There are so many details. If he could only figure out a way to streamline everything and get the same systems working for all, he could really free up his time for other things, reduce mistakes, and make more money.

Don't board members realize he's doing the best he can? Maybe he could get the board members to do more? Why do they keep bringing up the same issues all the time, anyway?

Reality Check

When board members work with property managers, it can be easy to view the property manager as a friend and not as a businessperson looking to help his own company. A condo association **pays** a property management company for its service. Therefore, a level of expectation needs to be met.

As a property manager, it's up to you to service the individual needs of a condo association according to the contract you signed. You need to be detailed enough that your information is accurate and you understand what's going on.

Board members expect you to do your job without constant follow-up. If the best you can do is below the standards established for servicing a property, your best isn't good enough.

If you discover an issue being brought up repeatedly, something is wrong with the communication. Perhaps you don't understand the underlying issue. Perhaps you have poor listening or questioning skills. Perhaps a resolution or decision is needed. Ignoring an issue will cause it to bubble up again in the future.

Expectations for a Property Manager

Condo board members expect a property manager to understand and manage their property, as though it were his own. They want clear, specific communication. They want questions instead of a property manager acting first and wanting permission later. They want a customer-service focus. They want to be consulted whenever necessary. They want efficiency, accuracy, and effectiveness as well as honesty and professionalism.

Mindset of a Business Owner

When you think about it, any property owner acts as a business owner of his property. He decides how and when to furnish, decorate, or remodel, according to his income and expenses. He may or may not need to consult with other family members beforehand.

For some reason, many board members don't necessarily view a condo association as a business. But, it is.

Reality Check

As a board member, you are responsible for the fiscal health of the association and the upkeep of the structure and common areas of the property. You need to have a long-term and a short-term strategy for accomplishing these tasks. You need to be clear about your purpose and mission. You need to feel empowered to get the results you seek. You cannot wish and hope that someone else will magically appear to resolve situations for you.

Income needs to be more than expenses. If it isn't, you need to figure out how to rectify the situation. You need to have a budget.

Although a condo association is typically a not-for-profit organization, you still need to factor in more income to cover future capital expenses, like a new roof, parking lot, or siding.

Mindset of a Neighborhood

Since condominium properties tend to be large, neighbor kids may view them as parks. They may feel they can use the property however and whenever they feel like using them.

Reality Check

Condo properties are not parks, of course. Unless you establish clear rules, be prepared for constant skirmishes. You may have to wait to back your car out, because the neighbor kids are playing. Maybe they become belligerent when confronted. Perhaps they even damage the property.

If you don't want trespassing, put signs up to that effect. Enlist the help of the police to stop all transgressions; otherwise, you will have neighborhood creep into your yard on a regular basis.

Chapter 2:

ASSOCIATION STRUCTURE

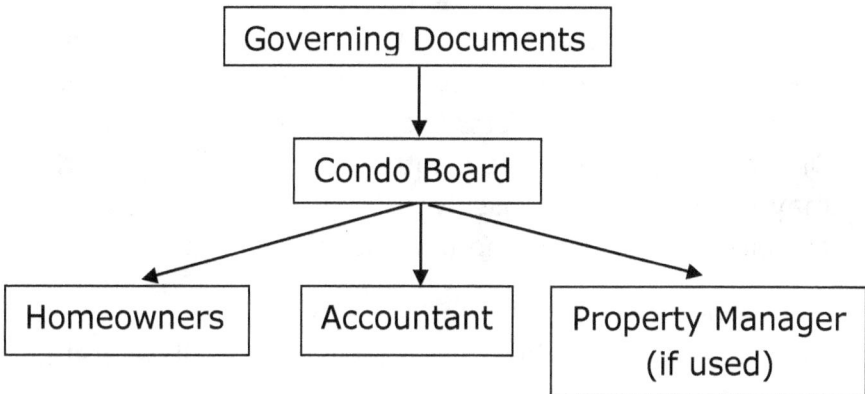

```
┌─────────────────────────────┐
│    Governing Documents      │
└─────────────────────────────┘
              │
              ▼
      ┌─────────────────┐
      │   Condo Board   │
      └─────────────────┘
      ╱        │        ╲
     ▼         ▼         ▼
┌──────────┐ ┌──────────┐ ┌──────────────────┐
│Homeowners│ │Accountant│ │ Property Manager │
│          │ │          │ │    (if used)     │
└──────────┘ └──────────┘ └──────────────────┘
```

This diagram shows a basic condo association structure. Other variations exist, which may include an attorney to handle legal matters. But for now, let's focus on the five parts as shown: governing documents, condo board, homeowners, accountant, and property manager.

Governing Documents

Governing documents are king in the condo world. They are the blueprints for what a condo property is, for what changes can be made, if any. They also describe the rules and regulations.

To make this description more interesting, imagine the governing documents as a bike. Each of the following documents make up one part of this bike.

Articles of Incorporation

Before you own and operate a bike, you need a receipt for payment and possibly, a bike license. Think of the Articles of Incorporation from a state's Secretary of State as a combination of that receipt and license. Without it, you can't legally operate as a condo association.

Along with a certificate, the Articles of Incorporation feature the association's legal name, its purpose, location, a description of members, the names of the first Board of Directors along with their authority, and how the articles may be amended or dissolved. The articles are signed by the incorporator and a notary public.

A purchase agreement used by first homeowners of the property may follow. This agreement details everything that's included in each condo unit.

The Articles of Incorporation have to be renewed annually with the state's Secretary of State. We have our accountant handle this whenever they file our taxes.

Declarations

You can think of the Declarations, otherwise known as the Covenants, Conditions, and Restrictions, as the bike frame. They support the entire condo association by providing the plans for the association. The Declarations are recorded in the county in which the property is located and are legally binding. Any amendments to this document would need to be recorded as well.

Typical components of the Declarations include:

- definitions

- parameters of a unit
- description of common elements
- description of limited common elements
- taxes and assessments
- voting rights of homeowners
- covenants and restrictions for use occupancy of the property
- plan for the association and administration of the condo
- common expenses and assessments
- insurance
- maintenance and repair
- declarant rights and covenants
- amendment and termination
- rights of first mortgagees
- miscellaneous

It is signed by the president and a notary public. A deed description, legal description, and diagram of the property typically follow the Declarations in the governing documents.

ByLaws

The bylaws act like the handlebars steering you to where you want to go. Within the bylaws, you'll find the rules and regulations, the brakes you need to prevent you from going too far.

Most answers a board member will need to govern the association are found here. You'll find:

- details of voting procedures
- meeting protocol
- board member responsibilities
- officer descriptions
- assessment protocol
- maintenance and repair issues
- rules of conduct

The articles of the bylaws are signed by the secretary.

Amendments

Any amendments or changes to the governing documents must be made according to the rules for that condo association. The rules stipulate the percentage of voting members needed to make an amendment.

MNCOIA and FHA

Although these documents are not part of the governing documents, they work in conjunction with them.

(MNCOIA) Minnesota Community Interest Act

This state statute supersedes whatever is in the governing documents for the state of Minnesota. Each state will have its own such act. Think of this act like the reflectors on your bike. You need them. You know they're there. But, you don't always pay attention to them.

Just be aware of what's in your state statute for condo associations. Check periodically to make sure nothing has changed.

(FHA) Federal Housing Administration

If you want condo homeowners in your association to be able to get an FHA loan, you'll need to make sure your association is FHA compliant.

Basically, you send in a lot of paperwork about your association to a designated FHA office. The rules change constantly, so always check on the requirements before you start this project. To keep current, you must send in a renewal package every two years, as of this writing.

Condo Board Members

Condo board members function much like the motor for an association. Without them, nothing would get done.

A typical officer slate includes:

- president
- vice president
- secretary
- treasurer
- member-at-large (optional)

The president conducts the meetings and ensures orders are executed. She serves as the official signer of documents.

The vice president acts as president when the president is absent.

The secretary takes minutes of all meetings and posts notices of when meetings will be held.

The treasurer works with the accountant regarding receipts, invoices, and all other money matters.

A member-at-large does not have an official job description. She simply serves as a board member or director.

Officers usually are volunteers. They can deduct mileage and unreimbursed expenses on their taxes, if itemized, as of this writing.

Meetings

Meeting notices are posted according to the required advance notice stated in the bylaws.

Generally, any condo homeowner can attend any meeting. Board members need to have an agenda and an understanding of how to conduct business efficiently and effectively. Although homeowners can attend, they cannot vote at board meetings and are not allowed to participate in discussions, unless authorized to do so by the board.

Generally, there are three types of meetings:

- <u>Board meetings</u> - when officers conduct business

- <u>Annual meeting</u> - when all homeowners meet to elect officers and to discuss pertinent condo business

- <u>Special meeting</u> - when a meeting of all homeowners is needed to discuss or vote on an urgent matter

Consult your bylaws to determine when and how you can set up each type of meeting.

Rule Enforcement

Board members enforce the rules, as outlined in the governing documents.. A business mindset can help a board member keep friendships at bay when enforcing rules. Violations occur because of a transgression of a documented rule in the governing documents, not because of someone's personal opinion as to a code of conduct.

All board members need to act in harmony with rule enforcement. Otherwise, a homeowner could play one board member against another.

Vendors

Board members collect bids from vendors: lawn care, snow plowing, construction, etc. The board determines the criteria to be used in the selection process. Only the board can authorize a vendor to do work for the association. The board approves payments of bills after work has been completed satisfactorily.

Insurance

Of course, you'll need to make sure there's a master policy for your association property. Make sure there's a liability clause for board members within your policy. It's best to deal with insurance agents who are familiar with associations.

Legal Representation

Whether you need help drafting an amendment, collecting a debt, or putting a lien on a unit, you'll need an attorney. Attorneys specialize; therefore, it's important that you get one who understands homeowner association issues.

If you keep open communication channels within your association and strive to be fair and consistent with everyone, you will minimize your legal needs.

If you do use an attorney, he will provide advice. The board still decides on how to act on that advice.

NATIONAL NIGHT OUT AND OTHER EVENTS

The board may opt to use some association funds for getting food, for instance, for an event like National Night Out. Board members need to be cautious here, since many times, condo associations tend to be underfunded rather than overfunded.

If the event is important to condo owners and enough condo homeowners attend, it can be worth the expense. Otherwise, consider donating supplies or not having the event altogether.

Property Management Company

Scrutinize the operating agreement before signing it. Board members need to be clear on expectations and exactly what is and is not covered by the contract.

A property management company may be full-service or provide an a la carte menu of options from which to choose. Before deciding on anything, board members need to consider what they truly need and if a particular property manager can service those needs in the way they want.

Board members direct the property manager, not vice versa, unless the board grants the property manager permission to do the board's job, too. Typically, a property manager will also be a signer on any association checking or savings accounts to facilitate deposits and money transfers, if the board approves this.

Don't assume a property manager knows all or is detail-oriented. Unless he treats your property as if it were his own, mistakes will likely occur. Consider some mistakes which have happened to us:

- The wrong vendor was paid for work done on the property.

- Addresses on the homeowner list were not all correct.

- Names on the homeowner list were not all correct.

- Once, we found a copy of our board minutes on the public Internet, which occurred when the property management company uploaded the document to their website.

- Not all meetings were attended as stipulated in the contract.

- Contrary to the board's request, a property management company paid a vendor in full before the work was even done.

- Frequently, the board has had to follow up repeatedly with a property manager in order to get answers to questions.

- Frequently, a property manager had not kept track of what was in our minutes.

- In the past, a property management company had posted a different association's governing documents on our website.

- The board could not get homeowner contact information from a property management company.

- More than once, a property management company had increased their management fees without telling the board beforehand.

- Frequently, the board found mistakes on the financials: a wrong account used or a payment missed.

- Etc.

The caveat is not that all property management companies should be avoided. The caveat is that if you are considering working with a property management company, you need to do a little research beforehand. Decide what you will and will not accept and go from there. I would encourage you to make sure that all important points are documented in the contract. And, hold the property management company accountable for their work. If you expect less, you'll probably get less.

The location of a property management company may matter as well. If it's located too far away from the condo property, they may charge an extra fee for a trip charge both ways. If the board uses them to work with vendors, every time they're on site or check on work, there will be a trip charge. You also can't count on a property manager being in attendance while a vendor works on site. If you have a property manager select vendors, his criteria may be different from yours.

Although a property manager usually oversees the completion of your financials, you can't assume the financials are accurate. Many times, they assume their accountant is accurate without double checking the work.

Property managers can have a high turnover rate. Don't count on the property management company to train the replacement manager. It's more likely the board will need to start the relationship from scratch.

The board pays a property management company a monthly agreed-upon fee, so long as an agreement is intact.

Accountant

I highly recommend that you have an accountant you trust do your financials. Some associations have a board member do the books. Bad idea. Even if that board member is honest and above reproach, the liability is too great. Besides, what happens if something happens to her or if she moves?

Financials

Typically, condo associations receive money from monthly dues or assessments from each homeowner, interest from any bank accounts, and any special assessments charged for projects like new garage doors. Every condo association should have an assessment collections policy detailing when dues are due, if and when a late fee applies, and how disputes are handled.

The condo board normally allocates monies received into at least two accounts: operations and capital or reserves.

Operations refer to any expense required for the general maintenance and upkeep of the property, like lawn care, snow plowing, electricity, water and sewer, building insurance, management or accounting fees, painting, caulking, cleaning, garbage and recycling, etc. Operations expenses basically maintain what's already there.

Capital or reserves refer to monies set aside for future capital expenses, like a new roof, new siding, new carpeting, new parking lot, new gutters, etc. Capital reserves are used to replace or upgrade an item.

Deciding how much money to put in each account can be a big deal. For instance, as of this writing, in Minnesota, once money is put into a capital reserve account, that money cannot legally be spent on anything other than a capital expense item. Money in an operations account can legally be used for either an operations or capital expense item. The challenge for any board is to make sure both accounts maintain enough money to manage the property without having to resort to on-the-spot special assessments.

Like most people, condo homeowners like to plan how their money will be spent. If a board intentionally underfunds the property, only to slap a large special assessment on unsuspecting homeowners later on, you can imagine the financial and emotional turmoil that would result for all concerned. Therefore, the board's job is not only proper collection and allocation of monies but good communication with all homeowners.

How does the board know what the financial position of an association is? For that answer, we look to four documents: a budget, balance sheet, income statement, and general ledger.

Budget

An annual budget denotes typical income, like monthly dues, and typical expenses, like lawn care, cleaning, etc. for each month of that year.

If a special project is anticipated for one year, each month could reflect 1/12 of the total project cost, for example.

It helps to put some thought into creating a budget that is practical. You really are limited by the amount of money your association takes in. Depending on the governing documents, you may or may not be able to invest any monies for the purpose of maximizing your return.

You can find a sample budget in the appendices.

Balance Sheet

A balance sheet is a statement of financial position for one month vs. the same month in the previous year. It depicts assets or any monies belonging to the association and which accounts they are located in. It also shows any liabilities, like loan amounts, which are owed. The liabilities are subtracted from the assets to show the net assets or equity for the association.

You can find a sample balance sheet in the appendices.

Income Statement

Any revenues or income appear at the top next to the budgeted amount and the year-to-date amounts. Each expense category and its amount is listed below the income section.

You can find a sample income statement in the appendices.

General Ledger

The general ledger shows the details of all transactions, including payments made to particular companies for services rendered.

Usually, the condo board members review all of the financial documents; however, when a homeowner wants to view the financials, typically, he gets a copy of the balance sheet and income statement. The budget can be included with the minutes at the time it is created.

At the end of the fiscal year, the accountant should file taxes. We also have her renew our corporation status with the Minnesota Secretary of State. That way we always keep current.

Condo Homeowners

First and foremost, condo homeowners are the board's customers. Even so, homeowners are expected to pay their dues and any special assessments on time, to obey the rules and regulations in the governing documents, and to communicate any issues to the board.

Chapter 3:

COMMUNICATION

Since a condo association can be a microcosm of what is seen at the national political level, effective communication is critical for achieving success. There are officers, authority, sometimes unhappy homeowners, sometimes botched communication, sometimes power struggles, issues regarding technology, and varying attitudes about how to handle money. Personalities can get in the way, if systems are not set in place to promote transparency and fairness. Sometimes a board member may look at a homeowner as a minion instead of realizing that a board member is in a *service* position, one whereby decisions need to be made for the greater good of the association.

By the same token, sometimes a homeowner forgets a board member is a volunteer. If homeowners don't respect a board member's time, for instance, the board member might not want to serve again. This is why it's crucial to have guidelines that work efficiently and effectively for all affected parties.

Communication starts with an approach. Board members need to set the tone by displaying an attitude of service. They don't need to grovel or submit to unrealistic expectations. Rather, they need to have a firm and confident understanding of their position and its boundaries. For instance, if the board makes the minutes easily accessible and a homeowner chooses to not read the minutes but expects a board member to update him personally on what's going on, that would be an unrealistic expectation of a board member's time. After all, if a board member had to verbally update each homeowner with whatever was already in the minutes, he wouldn't have time to do anything else.

When communicating with condo homeowners, vendors, or an accountant, the board has to always include three elements: legality, fairness, and consistency.

Legality

The board has to abide by the governing documents as well as any state statutes or local ordinances. A state statute might state how reserves should be handled, for instance. A local ordinance may define when late hours begin. For example, if late hours start at 10 p.m., you might not want your governing documents to stipulate 8 p.m. as the late hour start time. A late hour refers to when any loud or excessive noise should stop.

The board also needs to be aware of privacy concerns. For example, our governing documents state that unit numbers with any past-due amounts need to be included in the annual meeting packet. We do that. However, throughout the year, a homeowner may inadvertently miss a dues payment. It would serve no useful purpose to note the missed payment in the board minutes for that month. A far better way to handle it would be to contact the homeowner directly to alert him that the payment was missed and that, if your policy states this, a late fee will apply. Usually, if the missed payment was unintentional, the matter will be resolved quickly.

Unless already covered in your insurance policy or in the governing documents, you might want to create and have board members sign a conflict-of-interest agreement. Sometimes a board member has her own business. The board could opt to give special preference to that board member. Perhaps the board decides to not get other bids, for example, or to pay that member more than they should. To avoid a conflict of interest, it would be better to not hire a board member, if at all possible.

Fairness

The board needs to assess the fairness of its policies and communication. If a policy cannot be communicated clearly or enforced easily, then the policy needs to be re-worked or omitted.

For instance, when the board creates an assessment collections policy, these questions need to be answered:

- When is the assessment due?

- What happens if it's late?

- If a late fee is charged, how much will that be?

- What happens if it's never paid?

- When might a past-due account go to collections?

- Who would pay for the collections fee?

- Could a lien be put on a condo?

- If so, when would that take place?

You'll notice that each of these questions is very specific. The answers should be just as specific. Specificity leads to easy enforcement and, consequently, fairness, because the steps can be followed for each case of a past-due account.

Of course, every situation can't be categorized as neatly as for an assessment collections policy. A complaint procedure comes to mind. While the type of complaints may vary, you can create a policy for handling complaints that's fair as well.

For instance:

- How should a homeowner communicate a complaint to the board?

- When will the board address it?

- How and when can a homeowner appeal a decision?

- What happens next?

- When is the final outcome reached?

- How will the homeowner be notified?

For example, if there's a complaint lodged against another homeowner or a board member observes a rule infraction, you could try contacting the offending homeowner directly to let him know about the rule infraction. Maybe he didn't know or forgot some of the rules. If the homeowner persists in breaking the rules, the board needs to send a letter to that homeowner specifying what the infraction is and what you expect to happen, along with a deadline of compliance within two weeks, or a fine for each occurrence could be levied against him. If the homeowner has any objections, he would need to address them within that two-week period, should the matter get to this stage.

Again, specific questions will require specific answers. When something goes wrong, err on the side of having documentation, especially for chronic rule-breakers.

Consistency

If done correctly, as in the preceding examples, policies can be a board member's friend. They act like blueprints to guide you. If board members are diligent about following the governing documents, any policies, laws, and precedence, consistency will result. It's when board members disregard their blueprints and make decisions based on personal opinions or feelings that don't necessarily coincide with the best interests of the association, that they run into trouble with fairness, consistency, and, sometimes, legality.

For instance, if you have a rule about no pets in the building and a homeowner has a service animal, federal laws pertaining to service animals supersede any condo rules regarding no pets. Service animals are not considered as pets.

Or, maybe a board member doesn't like flowers on a patio and doesn't think anyone should have flowers. If there's no rule or law against them, that board member would be out of order to demand their removal.

Basically, board members need to communicate from a position of service. Their objectives in any situation are to understand and to get results. When they make decisions, they need to communicate them clearly. How might that be done? Read on...

Tools of Communication

Every condo association needs to meet at some point. The governing documents outline the minimum frequency for board meetings and the annual meeting and when notice has to be given. Every meeting requires minutes. Minutes need to be accessible to all homeowners.

Whether minutes are printed, emailed, or displayed some other way will depend on what is allowed in the governing documents.

Basically, an ideal board member would be rule-abiding, service-oriented, positive, responsive, pro-active on maintenance issues, trustworthy, and honest.

If you want to set your homeowners up for success, give them a welcome packet after they have moved in. This welcome packet should include the following:

- a list of board members' names and contact information
- current dues amount and how and when to make payments
- when board meetings are held and the minutes posted
- when garbage and recyclables are picked up, along with what is allowed and not allowed; specify that items like mattresses and furniture require an additional charge
- synopsis of important rules to follow

- copies of any policies not covered in the governing documents; for example, assessment collections policy, bylaws violation policy, complaint policy, water leak policy

I'd like to make a final note about renters. Board members are obligated to serve condo homeowners, not renters. If some condos can be rented in your association, it's the condo homeowner for the rented unit who is responsible for the tenant. That said, the communication boundary can blur quite easily.

If there's a water leak or some other emergency, it would be in a board member's best interests to take care of it quickly and to alert the condo homeowner, if not already done. Depending on the circumstances, the expense could be the homeowner's or the association's.

It's wise to know who the renters are, especially if your condo building has a locked lobby. If you happen to be at the front door and a stranger walks into the lobby, don't let him inside. Let the person he's coming to see buzz him in. That way, only people allowed in the building gain access to the building.

Chapter 4:

FINANCIAL GUIDELINES

The following guidelines have worked for our self-managed homeowners' association. If you ever have a property manager, you'll need to establish a checks-and-balance system for authorizing and verifying information in order to get your expected results. Some condo associations use a hybrid system, whereby the board members do some things, while delegating others to a property management company. Do whatever works for you. Just stay informed of what's going on in your association.

Bank

First, if you haven't done so already, you'll need to find a bank that suits your needs. Location matters, especially if board members have time constraints. The closer to your property, the better. Make sure they understand homeowner association concerns.

We have three accounts at our bank: one checking and two savings accounts. The checking and one of the savings accounts are designated as operations accounts. The second savings account is for capital reserves. Any dues or other assessments get deposited into the operations checking account. We have roughly 20% of our monthly revenue transferred from the operations checking account to the capital reserves account, where it stays until we need it for some future capital expenditure.

The operations savings account serves three purposes:

1. We earn some interest, however minuscule.

2. It acts as a buffer. We work to keep enough in the operations checking account for typical expenses, so that we don't need to dip into the operations savings account. If money ever needs to be transferred from it, there's an added step for accountability purposes.

3. If the amount in the operations checking account gets too large, we transfer some of it to the operations savings account. With a smaller, but adequate, amount of money in the operations checking account, homeowners are less inclined to want to "spend it all." Sometimes, a large amount of money makes some homeowners think it has to be spent, even if regular expense items have already been covered but future capital projects have not.

When you set up your accounts, you need to identify signers for those accounts. Certainly, the treasurer and your accountant would be good choices. Certainly, the board would need a signed agreement with the accountant as to what services she would provide and what the expectations would be. Have the accountant supply you with monthly bank statements when the financials are done. The board can then reconcile the statements to ensure accuracy.

Usually, best practices would suggest you not have the person writing the checks having access to the bank accounts. Technology has blurred the lines for what may be possible here, in some cases. For instance, we use bill pay from our checking account to pay vendors. I do not know of a way to have the checks created this way without a signature and have the checks sent to a board member to sign and then mail out. The extra steps would increase the possibility for errors.

Or, if a board member accessed the bill-pay system to create checks, that board member would also be a signer on the bank account and a volunteer at that. Either way, the person creating the checks has access to the bank account.

We believe we are working with an accountant we can trust. That said, we believe we also have enough checks and balances in place to spot any potential errors.

I would strongly advise that you don't have a board member as the accountant. There is also no need for every board member to be a signer for the bank accounts. The simpler, the better. Make sure when you get a copy of the signer sheets from the bank that there are no social security numbers listed. You won't want to be responsible for having that information in your possession.

Accountant

Once you've selected a good accountant, make her job easier and keep your costs lower by restricting access to board members only. If homeowners get used to contacting board members about any concerns, rather than the accountant, the board will be better informed about what needs to happen to address homeowners' issues more effectively. You know what they say about too many cooks in the kitchen.

We have our accountant do financials monthly; that is: a balance sheet, an income statement, and a general ledger. We have monthly board meetings and ask that the financials be done prior to the board meeting, so we can review them. The accountant also includes a copy of the bank statements. I'll highlight what to look for under the board meeting subheading in this chapter.

When it comes to auditing financials, obviously this is preferable. A self-managed association with limited resources, however, may choose to forego that expense and rely on their own careful financial reviews instead.

Recordkeeping

Every business keeps track of records. Your condo association should be no different. It never hurts to be somewhat redundant. Yes, your accountant should have copies, electronic or otherwise, of all information they receive. HOWEVER, we have had a past accountant "lose" many of our records. Therefore, my recommendation is to keep hard copies of financials, minutes, invoices, and any other pertinent information, as well as electronic copies of the same.

That way, nothing gets "lost" and board members can access the information easily either for themselves or for a homeowner.

Dues Collection

Give all homeowners the option of having their monthly dues automatically withdrawn. You can give them a copy of the direct debit authorization form from the bank. Give homeowners the option of giving the form directly to the accountant to input. Or, they can put the form in an envelope for a board member to deliver to the accountant.

Our dues are due the first of each month; however, we have a grace period until the 15th. The grace period means anyone who pays their dues on or before the 15th of the month will not be charged a late fee. This stipulation was grandfathered in from previous procedures. It actually creates more work for the board, though, as you'll soon see.

We assess a late fee of $15 for each monthly dues amount not paid on time. As of this writing, we have no homeowners behind on paying their dues.

In order to treat dues collection like a business and not have it be dependent on any one board member, we purchased a P. O. box strictly for association business. We also have an association mailbox inset in the first-floor hallway of our building. Homeowners may drop their dues in the association mailbox or send them to the P. O. box. Vendors also send their invoices electronically or to the P. O. box. All of our board members have keys to the association and P. O. mailboxes.

At the end of each year, we order coupon books for homeowners wishing to pay by check. For some, this helps them keep track of when they need to pay.

Certainly, you can work toward automating your system by charging an additional fee for check handling. Chances are, an extra charge would convince check writers to have their dues payments automatically withdrawn from their accounts.

Dues Collection System

I have a manila folder that I use solely for dues and invoices. First, I created a simple grid. The top of the left-most vertical column has the year. Other vertical columns show the months of January through December. Each horizontal row shows a unit number. (See Appendix.)

For any homeowner automatically withdrawing their dues, I write "AW" in the squares for that unit, January through December. When I receive a dues payment, I put a check mark in the square for that month. If a late fee was applied, I put a "+" after the check mark in the same square.

This grid serves as a checks-and-balance system against whatever the accountant might show.

I check the association mailbox daily. I pay particular attention just before and just after the first of the month as well as on the 15th. I end up going to the bank at least four times every month.

After I collect the checks, I:

1. print a copy of them with 3 to a page.

2. write the dues' month and unit number by each check copy.

3. write which bank account to use to pay the vendor on any invoices.

4. sign and date the marked-up invoices.

5. print a copy of the marked-up invoices.

6. deposit the checks at the bank to the appropriate condo association account.

7. staple the deposit slip to the copy of the checks.

8. give the check copies with deposit slip and any marked-up invoices to the accountant to process.

9. show the invoice copies to other board members at the next board meeting.

This system can be used by any board member. It establishes transparency, accuracy and accountability and is easy to do.

Special Assessments

Special assessments can occur for a couple of reasons. Say, new garage doors are needed. Typically, garage doors are a limited common element, in this case, a homeowner expense. Since some degree of uniformity is expected on condo property, the board would normally oversee the project and collect the monies.

You might think association funds should be used, because all homeowners are included. The operations account takes care of typical routine expenses. New garage doors would be something special; hence, a special assessment.

Of course, the board could arrange a payment schedule for homeowners to make the expense easier to handle. When we do this, we do not charge interest; however, late fees would apply, whenever deadlines are not met.

To get a better handle on special assessments and maintenance costs, it would be good to get a reserve study done. Professionals doing reserve studies determine a timeline for future maintenance items as well as the expected costs for each. Based on that, they calculate how much money needs to be in the reserves to fund those projects adequately.

Again, self-managed associations having limited resources may not be able to afford this expense. Typically, it is thought precious resources should be spent directly on maintenance items rather than on plans to address maintenance items.

Reserve studies can provide a very beneficial road map, however. Board members may or may not have the expertise or the detail orientation needed to do a good job creating a workable plan on their own.

Whether professionally done or not, a board needs to create some type of plan to keep the fiscal health of a property intact.

Another reason the board may charge a special assessment is when a cost needs to be reimbursed to the association. The more accurate term here would probably be reimbursement rather than special assessment.

For instance, say a homeowner's visitor had muck on his shoes when he walked on the hallway carpet. If the board has to have the area where he walked cleaned by a professional carpet cleaner, the association would pay for that expense initially, since the board requested the vendor's work. This arrangement also preserves the board-vendor relationship.

After the board receives the invoice, they pay the invoice and instruct the accountant to invoice the unit involved for the same amount, unless the board has agreed upon some type of installment system. Then multiple invoices would be sent to the homeowner over time with the sum total equaling the total charge for the carpet cleaning.

Whenever the board assesses a fine for noncompliance of the rules and regulations, that would also be considered a special assessment. You should have some type of policy pertaining to fine assessment to ensure fairness and accountability.

You could designate a specific dollar amount for all fines. You could specify a dollar range for the fine. Or, you could leave it at the board's discretion, in which case, someone would need to keep track of precedence to ensure fairness.

A lesser fine would work better for smaller infractions than a greater fine. Chances are, if you work toward creating working relationships with the homeowners, you'll be able to resolve most situations without having to consider a fine.

Board Meetings

Check your governing documents, so you're in compliance with when and how board meetings should work.

We hold monthly board meetings in the evening in a board member's unit. They can be held anywhere. You have to provide sufficient, advance notice, so any homeowner who wants to attend may do so.

We have a bulletin board at the front and back entrances. Both show the upcoming meeting notice. Only the front bulletin board also has board members' contact information as well as the latest minutes.

We believe it's easier to stay on top of what's going on with regular meetings. Some are very short. Others are longer, depending on the circumstances. In either case, remember that a board is not a social club. The association is a business. Treat it as such. Don't let personal or social issues derail your meetings. You can be friendly without having to be friends.

To give board members time to prepare for a meeting, the secretary should email the agenda to the board members 4-5 days prior to the board meeting. Any board member may add items to the agenda.

If a homeowner comes to a board meeting, he or she is first on the agenda. A homeowner can observe the rest of the meeting, if desired, but cannot partake in it.

The board considers several financial elements at a board meeting. The prior month's financials received from the accountant have to be reviewed. If one board member gets the financials via email beforehand, that member then forwards them to the other board members immediately for their review. Financials include the balance sheet, income statement, general ledger, and bank statements.

One thing to note here is that board meetings are for decision making. The way to do that in a timely manner is to make sure all board members get all pertinent information BEFORE the board meeting. That way, each board member can review the material at her leisure. She can then go to the board meeting prepared to ask questions, discuss items in an informed manner, and make decisions accordingly.

Back to the financials review.... You can find a sample budget, a sample balance sheet, and a sample income statement in the appendices.

Some things to pay attention to on the balance sheet:

- Are there sufficient funds in the operations checking account to pay for upcoming bills?

- Are the capital reserves on track to pay for future capital projects?

- Did the capital reserves amount increase by the transferred amount indicated on the income statement?

- Can an amount be transferred from operations checking to operations savings?

- Did the operations checking account increase or decrease by the net income amount on the income statement, compared with last month's operations checking account amount?

Some things to pay attention to on the income statement:

- Do expense amounts match invoices received?
- How do the expense items compare with the budgeted amounts?
- Was the net income positive or negative?
- If negative, is this a one-time event, or does it suggest a future trend?
- Were expense items put in the correct categories?
- Are any expense amounts unusual or incorrect?
- Are any known expense items for this time period not shown?

Some things to pay attention to in the general ledger:

- Does the general ledger display transactions accurately?
- Were the correct companies paid?
- Are invoices being paid on time?

If the board is satisfied with the financials, someone needs to move to approve the financials. Another has to second the motion. A vote records the number of yeas vs. nays.

If approved (usually by a majority or one over half), a board member needs to email that approval to the accountant. Any proposed changes or questions also need to be sent to the accountant. If the financials aren't approved at the board meeting, they can be approved via email after any questions or concerns have been addressed (if your governing documents allow this).

At a board meeting, the board also reviews invoices and vendor bids.

Sometimes a board member buys supplies for the association and is then reimbursed for that expense. These supplies may include snow salt, shovels, light bulbs, etc.

Here is the system for handling reimbursements:

- Vote to approve spending money for a supply item.

- Purchase the item and provide a receipt.

- Make a copy of the receipt and indicate who should be reimbursed along with her address. Sign and date the sheet.

- Give the sheet to the accountant for processing.

Taxes and Corporate Filing

Have the accountant do the taxes at the end of the fiscal period, usually a calendar year. At the same time, have her renew the association's corporate filing with the state's Secretary of State.

With financial systems in place, the board will have an easier time keeping track of the fiscal picture of the condo property.

Chapter 5:

OPERATIONS GUIDELINES

You will find some overlap here with the financial guidelines in the previous chapter. I have tried to keep this repetition to a minimum.

New Homeowners

To build a sense of community, you need to welcome new homeowners. All board members should introduce themselves. Encourage them to contact you, if the need should arise.

If the homeowner doesn't already have a copy of the governing documents, email him a copy. It wouldn't hurt to give him a welcome packet highlighting important details like when garbage and recyclables are picked up, where dues are sent, and what the rules and regulations are. No one likes to be admonished first and then told what the rules are. You want to set each homeowner up for success.

This would be an excellent time to find out if he wants to automatically withdraw dues or pay by check and to exchange contact information.

Board Members

Make your contact information available to homeowners. We post our latest board minutes on a bulletin board by the front entrance next to the contact information. For homeowners not living on the premises, the secretary should email herself and bcc the landlords with a copy of the latest approved minutes and the latest approved balance sheet and income statement in PDF format.

If anything new happens on the property, post a notice by the front and back doors. Board members pre-approve any posted notices. Notices may pertain to work being done on the property to items not allowed in the recycling bin or to anything unusual that residents should be aware of. You cannot go wrong with greater communication. Indicate the notice is from the board and date it. A few days later, after residents have had a chance to read it, take it down.

Board Meeting Agenda and Minutes

You will find a sample agenda and sample minutes in the appendices.

The board makes decisions using Robert's Rules of Order in an informal way. Any time money is spent, someone has to move that, another has to second the motion, and all have to vote on that motion. All motions have to be recorded in the minutes.

Actually, board minutes only need to include the members present and absent, when the meeting was called to order, any motions, next meeting date/time/place, when the meeting was adjourned, and the secretary's name. This is what I call the bare-bones version. You'll find a sample of this in the appendices.

The problem with the bare-bones version is that homeowners like a little more substance. Knowing the methodology and reasons behind decisions helps to explain not only what happened in the meeting but how the board is looking at things overall. I call this version the expanded version. You'll find a sample of the expanded version in the appendices as well.

Some reasonable expectations about what to include in the minutes follow:

- Include just enough information so that homeowners understand the gist of what is being done.

- Do not violate privacy issues by including personal information or comments.

- If there is disagreement on the board about an issue, include how members think. Board members are elected. Including this information gives homeowners a sense of where each board member stands.

- Be forthcoming with good news as well as bad, so long as no rules are violated with sharing the information.

The secretary is responsible for providing a draft of the minutes to other board members as promptly as possible. Once approved, she has to promptly post the minutes for all homeowners to view.

Annual meeting minutes can be approved at the next annual association meeting, provided a quorum of homeowners is present. In fact, in order to conduct business at a board meeting, a quorum is needed there as well.

Filing System (Electronic and Hard Copy)

I recommend redundancy with your filing system. No business should have to depend on only one person or one system. Some homeowners may not be adept with computers or even have a computer. These folks would much prefer hard copies.

There are probably as many ways to set up a filing system as there are people. Whatever works for you should be the one you use. Think about what you're always digging for, and create a system to make items more easily accessible.

You'll definitely want to keep copies of financials, minutes, policies, vendor bids, and invoices. One way is to develop a record retention policy that states which records are kept where and in what format and for how long.

This can be problematic with self-managed associations. Resources are limited. An association may not have a website. Storage room on the premises may not be sufficient. Board members who have copies, electronic or otherwise, need to grant access to other homeowners upon request.

Vendors and Bids

You need to determine which projects you need bids for at a board meeting. Then, a board member contacts x number of companies for the bid. I recommend a minimum of 3 bids. Too many and you waste everyone's time. Too few and you don't get an accurate representation of what's out there. And, if you rely on just one or two, if they don't work out for you, you're down to zero.

The number of bids can also depend on the size and scope of the project. If a piece of a wooden bench needs to be fixed, just get a handyman, not a construction company. If you need new siding, then a construction company would be appropriate. Because of the cost involved, at least three, if not more, bids would be appropriate, depending on the size of your buildings.

When dealing with vendors, ask for:

- a current insurance certificate.

- a license number, where applicable.

- references.

- their work availability.

Remember that vendors work for you, the board, not the other way around. Some of them may not know how homeowners' associations work. You can save yourself a lot of frustration by having one point person on the board who deals with vendors. Any other board member can be involved throughout. Certainly, all board members need to be involved with any major decision. But having a point person streamlines the communication process. The vendor knows whom to contact. The point person keeps the board informed. Other homeowners, who aren't on the board, and any tenants should not be directing activities of a vendor. The board has fiscal responsibility for the property; therefore, only the board should direct vendors.

When getting bids, keep in mind that this is a confidential process. It would be unethical, and at times illegal, to trade information with competitors about each other's bids. If you ask vendors to give you their best offers first, you can avoid future headaches. Trying to nickel and dime a vendor defeats the whole purpose of establishing a steady, working relationship. By all means, hold vendors accountable, but be fair and realistic about the process.

A good working relationship involves more than just price. Other key factors include trust, integrity, flexibility, availability, and expertise. If something is wrong, would you trust this vendor to tell you? If something doesn't need to be done, would you trust this vendor to let you know that as well?

Handling Homeowners, Renters, and Complaints

Again, integrity is key. So are policies. Make sure you have a complaint policy.

Be fair. Be consistent. Focus on the issue, not the personality. Expect the same in return. Everyone likes to make the board accountable. That's fine. Yet, homeowners and any renters need to be accountable for their actions as well.

Again, consistency and fairness matter. You were probably looking for some type of sexy, magic bullet here.

I'm afraid good, old-fashioned, basic interpersonal communication skills rule. Easy to understand. Not always so easy to execute.

Steady efforts to use the governing documents as a blueprint and to follow existing policies should keep the personality out of the equation. It's not about the board member. It's about the board member doing her job. It's not about whether or not you like a homeowner. It's about what his concern is and how you can help him.

Along with this, it's a good idea to never create a rule you can't enforce. If you do this, you will be setting the stage for all sorts of future conflicts.

Handling Keys

We have keys to:

- building entrances.

- plumbing and electrical closets.

- the association mailbox.

- our P. O. mailbox.

The mailbox keys that each board member has were covered previously.

We have the plumbing and electrical closets keyed the same way. Each board member has this key. We also have a lockbox on one of the door handles. That way, if a board member is not on the premises, and a homeowner has a water or electrical issue, he can get into the closet by plugging in the code on the lockbox to get the key.

We also have a different lockbox inset in the wall in our front vestibule. Only the fire department has a key to this lockbox. This lockbox offers homeowners the option to add a copy of their unit key to the lockbox for emergency situations. If a homeowner decides to add a key or gets a new key, he calls the fire department to meet one of their people in the vestibule. Then, the homeowner can witness his key being put in the lockbox.

All homeowners have a building entrance key, of course. The board keeps the key card that's used to make additional keys. We have a locksmith make five additional keys at a time. If a homeowner wants another key, he has to pay for the cost of making that key. The board member then deposits that money in the operations checking account. The accountant will deduct that amount from a line item called "prepaid keys" on the balance sheet.

If you can find a reliable plumber you can trust, you might consider giving him a building key, just in case there's a leak and no board members are on site. You would need to give him the code to the plumbing closet as well.

As technology improves, you will have many more options for key access to your building. Every system has pros and cons. Do your due diligence to find what will work the best for you at a cost you can afford.

FHA (Federal Housing Administration)

If you want homeowners to have the option of getting an FHA loan to buy their units, you need to make sure the association is FHA compliant. My goal is not to detail every item needed here, because requirements can change yearly. You can always look up the latest requirements on the Internet or contact the FHA for clarification.

As of this writing, you need to renew your FHA status every two years to stay in compliance. You can save yourself some money by doing this work yourself. Otherwise, it could cost up to $1,000 or more to have someone else do it.

Setting Up a Maintenance Schedule

For routine items, it's best to set up a maintenance schedule. Then, just follow it.

For instance:

- clean the common areas every week.

- professionally clean the carpeting every spring and fall.

- clean dryer vents every other year.

- check emergency lights, smoke alarms, and fire extinguishers every year.

- do a spring walkthrough to create a punch list of needed fixes every year. Include any caulking, painting, and repair issues.

- do any other item you need to do.

Condo Association History

One thing that takes a bit of effort but comes in handy many times over is a condo association history. Instead of having to dig through boxes of records to find out when you last purchased something, just create a spreadsheet.

We keep track of the history using these columns: date, company name, item, cost, and any notes. On the same spreadsheet, we have a summary of what the dues are for each year. Another tab shows the term of office for each board member, so we know who is up for re-election at the annual meeting.

SUMMARY

That's about it. Thank you for serving on your board or for considering the endeavor. As you have seen, there is a time commitment for serving a homeowners' association. I know time is precious. But, someone has to do it, right? Who better than you, especially since you likely own one of the units in your association.

Good communication really is key. I can't stress that enough. The better your communication is, the more included your homeowners will feel. If you treat your homeowners well, your job on the board will be much easier.

Hopefully, I have given you enough information to make your job even smoother than it would have been otherwise. Should you have any questions, feel free to contact me at jewel@jewelpickert.com.

Good luck to you and to your association!

ACKNOWLEDGMENTS

This book would not be in its present form if it weren't for the detailed, insightful review by Toby Madden, a broker and property manager who owns Minnesota Nice Properties. Deb Svien, a fellow board member, also took the time to review this book and to offer comments to help me present the material in the best possible way for you, the reader. Thank you both for your efforts!

I would like to thank CreateSpace for their cover design of this book. Also, dream_books at fiverr.com gets the credit for the interior design, which makes it easy for you to read. While I am a writer, graphic elements are not my strong suit; therefore, they both saved me a lot of time. And both were very easy to work with. Thank you again.

APPENDICES

Glossary

Amendment - an addition or change to a motion or a governing document

Annual Meeting - a meeting at which a quorum of condo homeowners is expected to attend to conduct business and to elect officers

Article - a section of a governing document

Articles of Incorporation - a legal document from a state's Secretary of State, which designates a condo association as a corporation or business entity

Association - the term used to describe a group of condo homeowners belonging to a given Articles of Incorporation

Balance Sheet - a statement of assets and liabilities for a fixed period of time

Bid - a proposal submitted by a vendor to do business with a condo association

Board - a group of elected condo homeowners who manage the condo property

Budget - a snapshot of expected proposed expenses and income for a specified period of time

Bylaws - the rules and regulations for a condo association

Capital Expense - an expense on a new or replacement item, like a new roof, new gutters, new parking lot, new carpeting, new siding, etc.

Common Element - an area used by all condo homeowners, which is maintained with association funds, like a hallway, stairwell, or vestibule.

Condominium - a legal designation for a unit owned by an individual, which is part of a larger condo association

Contractor - vendor

Declarations - the Covenants, Conditions, and Restrictions for a condo property that are recorded at the county and are legally binding

Director - another term for board member

FHA - Federal Housing Administration -- created within the Department of Housing and Urban Development (HUD) in 1934 to jumpstart and to regulate the housing industry (according to HUD)

General Ledger - a detailed accounting of expenses and income which shows the account number, the entity involved, and any money transfers for each transaction

Governing Documents - the legal documents serving as the foundation upon which an association is based

Income Statement - a report detailing all expenses and revenue for a fixed time period against the budget and last year's amounts

Limited Common Element - an area which could be considered the responsibility of the homeowner or the association to maintain, like a patio, window, or garage door

MNCOIA - Minnesota Community Interest Act, a statute covering homeowners' associations

Operations Expense - an expense for repair or maintenance of an existing item

Property Management Company - a company in business to manage properties

Proxy - a form a homeowner can fill out and submit to the board to count toward the quorum total if the homeowner is unable to attend an annual meeting. The board, or a person designated by the homeowner, can vote on the homeowner's behalf.

Punch List - a to-do list of maintenance items for the condo property

Quorum - a number of homeowners needed to be present or via proxy at an annual meeting in order to conduct business; typically, a majority (as outlined in the governing documents, though)

Reserves - savings

Rules & Regulations - the list of what a homeowner can and cannot do within the association and is usually located within the bylaws

Vendor - a company or contractor who does work on the property for the association

12 Tips & Tricks for Self-Managed Associations

Let's address that intangible people part that tends to upend associations first.

1) **Avoid politics.** If you like politics, run for the city council. Run away from a homeowner's association. Too much is at stake with a person's home to elevate your cause above the interests of the association homeowners.

2) **Challenge yourself to accept people, but confront issues.** This can be particularly difficult to do, but the effort is worthwhile. A person is whoever he is. Don't waste time trying to re-make him to your specifications. Do try to steer everyone on a like-minded path of tackling any issues at hand. Every person's opinion should be valued and considered on its merit and feasibility. What some people don't realize is that some frustration or tension with the process is part of a democratic approach which can lead to better results.

   The motto is to confront issues by dealing with egregious behaviors, not by focusing on personalities.

3) **Avoid nepotism.** Strive to elect people based on their qualifications, not on their lineage. Strive to hire people based on the best fit for the property, not on their connection to a board member.

4) <u>Establish a tie-breaking system.</u> It means if you don't have an odd number of board members in attendance, what will you do? Does someone get more than one vote? Do you simply hash it out to an agreement? You decide.

5) <u>Do what's in the best interests of the association or property ALWAYS.</u> This should be obvious.

6) <u>Establish a checks-and-balance system.</u> Your bylaws should help with this. Follow them religiously. Every board member is expected to learn about their declarations, bylaws, financial, and legal issues. No one board member should be granted absolute, undue authority on anything. Make sure the majority of the board, unless otherwise noted in the bylaws, makes the decisions. Sometimes you'll agree; sometimes you won't. Abide by the majority decision anyway.

7) <u>Communicate openly with homeowners.</u> Transparency is your friend. It douses idle speculation. Communicate openly about meetings, policies, issues, and, especially, money. If you don't, you will be stuck in the hallway repeating yourself to everyone you meet. You might improve your communication skills that way; however, your time management will suffer.

8) <u>Document everything, and keep all records.</u> It's simple. Misunderstandings disappear quickly when you can whip out documentation to support your claim. If nothing else, it keeps our memories sharp.

9) **Get at least 3 bids for important projects.** This takes time. Remember step 5? It's in the best interests of the association. When you do find contractors you trust, stick with them. The 3-bid rule is no longer applicable for them, unless something changes.

10) **Establish a budget and adequate reserves.** It's difficult to know if you've arrived, if you don't even know where you're headed; hence, the importance of a budget. Without adequate reserves, you will be limited in which projects can be addressed.

11) **Save for future capital projects.** This ties into step 10. Some people have never seen this kind of money before and believe it has to be spent, because there's so much of it. "Much," of course, is a relative term; especially, when you realize the costs of capital projects are beyond your financial capacity to fulfill them.

12) **Manage your time.** With only 24 hours in a day, a board position can morph into a part-time or full-time, unpaid job. With so many other personal commitments to attend to, a board member may come to resent the necessary or expected time commitment. If board members all pitch in to help, no one person bears the whole burden.

One particular time drainer is dealing with complaints. In this case, homeowners may come to resent the bearer of bad or unpleasant news.

If time management or other issues become too overwhelming, you could always hire a property management company to help out. Just remember to get at least 3 bids.

(previously published in *Minnesota Community Living*, a Minnesota Chapter Community Associations Institute publication)

Renters & Owners Demystified

In the never-ending renter vs. owner debate, each is
viewed as a mysterious creature by the other. Owners
believe renters don't care about the property and
violate the most rules. Renters, on the other hand, think
owners don't treat them equally. After all, they live here,
too.

First, let's debunk the first myth. I have to say that in
my condo building, the absolute worst rule offender ever,
to date, was a previous owner. He's "previous" for a
reason. It could be that for most owners, enough time has
passed to get them on board with following the rules, so
normally renters stand out in comparison. Because of
renters' transient nature, rule education is constant. I still
think that if the board strives to let renters succeed
through consistent communication with the landlords, a
win-win atmosphere could be enjoyed by all.

We all experience transitions in our lives. For many
renters, this state brings its own challenges. I believe
renters really do prefer to belong to a community rather
than to be thought of as outcasts.

Renters need to understand, however, that they are
part of a "shared" community. They have to be sensitive to
their impact on others and act accordingly lest they
perpetuate a negative perception. Like any newbies, they
might have to work a bit harder to fit in and to gain the
trust of other residents.

Renters need to also realize owners are primarily
accountable to other owners. Owners pay the association

dues. If all owners are expected to deal with all renters, the owners' time commitment would increase exponentially. We all know how precious someone's time is. We don't want to squander it unnecessarily. That's what boards and management companies are for: taking care of issues.

Owners know renters don't have the same vested interest in their property. Renters don't own the deed or title to their properties. They don't get to vote at meetings. An unequal status does exist by virtue of the established business arrangement. Sometimes, owners need to be thankful that their building's units are occupied though.

Nevertheless, common courtesy, consistency, and fairness go a long way in helping all residents acclimate to the expectations and machinations of their property. A little bit of earned trust and respect on both sides can decrease rule violations, increase security, and foster rapport.

Eventually, owners and renters will see that each is not so mysterious after all.

(previously published in *Minnesota Community Living*, a Minnesota Chapter Community Associations Institute publication)

R & R Does Not Stand For Rest & Relaxation

Common sense just isn't all that common when dealing with rules and regulations. It's not that people don't try to do the right thing or don't know what the right thing might be. It's just that individuals have their own perspectives based on a lifetime of experiences. In a sense, each one of us interprets common sense differently.

How about when people move in during the winter and prop the outside door of a condo building open the whole time they're driving back and forth from their previous residences? Maybe they think it's easier for them to not open and close the door constantly. It doesn't occur to them that it's colder for everyone else in the building.

Or when someone parks perpendicular to the garages and blocks another's access to the garage? Surely, common sense would prevail. After all, who wants to have to ask permission to get into or out of the garage? Again, it means the parkers have to think of how their actions impact others. The perspective might be it just takes them a minute. I've noticed these people typically have very long minutes, sometimes even extending to an hour or more.

All is not lost, however. People can surprise you and do the kindest things for others. It's just that when it comes to their daily routines, that "other" concept can become hidden.

How can boards manage rules and regulations effectively? Make sure each rule is feasible, simple, specific, measurable, and enforceable.

Feasible. Does the rule make sense? If not, why are you trying to enforce this? If someone jumps over the patio railing to access the condo through the patio doors instead of entering through the front door, would preventing that be a feasible rule? That's akin to saying you have to enter the building through the back door instead of the front. Why bother with this? So long as the bylaws show patios as limited common elements, any subsequent damage from this practice would conceivably be paid for by the homeowner.

Simple. If you need a lawyer to interpret your rule, it's too complex. If it's too complex, homeowners won't be able to follow it, let only understand it. For example, stating "owners need to be quiet whenever someone is sleeping unless they know they're awake and always for each of the holidays and weekends" is way too complex, and, of course, not even feasible. It would be better to simply follow whatever the city's noise ordinance stipulates. That way you have a specific time period people can adhere to.

Specific. Dues are due by the first of each month. If received after the 10th day of the same month, a late fee of $20 will be charged for that month and for every subsequent month in which the dues are late. Pretty specific. A homeowner knows the exact parameters and consequences of non-compliance. Is your assessment policy this specific?

Measurable. Do homeowners know when they're in non-compliance? Let's say that when there is a minimum snowfall of 2", vehicles have to be moved to a plowed spot after the snow plow makes its first pass. A visual cue and the weather reports will confirm the 2" designation. Although it can be difficult to know exactly when the plow will come, it's easy to figure out when it has been there. If the rules say a vehicle in non-compliance can get towed, then it should come as no surprise when that happens.

Enforceable. Since board members typically are the rule enforcers, it makes no sense to make rules that irritate others simply because they aren't enforced or are incapable of being enforced. Fairness matters. Homeowners may not say anything, but they notice when rules are misapplied or not applied. So long as rules are enforced fairly and consistently, there likely won't be much pushback to the board. Yes, some people try to push through boundaries. It's in their nature. Rein them in, and, at least, they'll know that rules mean something and aren't arbitrary.

Consider this example. A homeowner suggests a loading/unloading only parking spot by the front door. No permanent parking is to be allowed there. Is it feasible? On its face, it might seem to be helpful to everyone. Is it simple? Perhaps. Specific? Maybe 15 minutes is allotted for that loading spot. Measurable? Perhaps, although, someone would have to time each parked vehicle from start to finish. Therefore, enforceability would be extremely difficult. Who has the time to monitor such a thing? We all know how the honor system works. It doesn't.

Common sense may not be all that common. But, the procedure for creating rules should be. If a board gets too rule happy, the members will be stuck with endless enforcement issues. If people keep complaining about a rule, it may be a sign to look closer at its legitimacy. Or, if legitimate, it's time the board made it clear the rule isn't changing. Otherwise, homeowners will have you endlessly modifying everything. In that type of situation, it would be difficult to even get people to want to serve on the board.

(previously published in *Minnesota Community Living*, a Minnesota Chapter Community Associations Institute publication)

Due Process With Complaints

Everyone has different ideas regarding acceptable behavior. In my college years, I had a roommate who had exceptional hearing. Our off-campus apartment was on the second floor. She constantly complained about the noise downstairs. I could never hear anything. In fact, when I put my ear to the carpeted floor, I barely heard a sound. But, it was deafening to her. I discovered she always had a perfectly quiet environment in which to fall asleep in her younger years; hence, the exceptional hearing.

Board members can do a few things to streamline a complaint procedure that's fair to all.

Get specifics.

Whenever someone complains, ask all pertinent questions, so the issue can be addressed in its entirety the first time. Who did what? When did they do this? What did they do? How did it affect you? Many times you won't know why, unless you're a mind reader. I know I'm not.

Document the complaint.

Document the complaint in an email to other board members and the management company, if applicable. Stick to the facts. Avoid unnecessary gossip with other owners. Avoid smear and whisper campaigns. An association is a business. Conduct yourselves as professionally as possible.

Establish a step policy of enforcement.

If you don't already have a policy in place, develop one now. Make it easy to be consistent. After the initial complaint documentation, perhaps a courtesy phone call is in order. Agree on a timeline until each subsequent step occurs. If non-compliant after a specified period from the complaint documentation, then what? Perhaps another phone call or a letter or a fine? The board needs to decide this. If non-compliant after another specified time period, then what again? A letter, a fine, or something else? It's important to increase the repercussions incrementally to gain compliance.

Whatever you state you will do, you must do; otherwise, your credibility vanishes. Your follow through is paramount.

Communicate policy with homeowners.

Although obvious, I'll state it anyway. Any policy put in place by the board needs to be communicated to the homeowners. There should be no secrets here. Make it a win for the homeowners by letting them know what your expectations for compliance are. If you're in doubt on any aspect of your policy, never fear. The homeowners will let you know about any inconsistencies. That's their job.

(previously published in *Minnesota Community Living*, a Minnesota Chapter Community Associations Institute publication)

Policy Creation Guidelines

Since each association is different, I provide the following information to give you some ideas of what would need to be considered for each of these types of policies, if you don't already have them.

Assessment Collections Policy

- Decide when your dues are due.

- What, if any, late fee will be applied, if not paid by the deadline?

- How will the homeowner know he is late?

- If non-payment continues into the next month, what will happen?

- How will all homeowners know of your policy?

- Is there a point at which a non-payment would go to collections?

- Who would do the collections?

- When will this policy begin?

Complaint Policy

- How does a homeowner contact the board with a complaint?

- What is the turnaround time for the board to respond to the homeowner?

- What are the expectations of the homeowner?

- Do any of the governing documents or policies cover the complaint in question?

- When will the board member consult with other board members about the issue?

- When will the final decision be made as to how to handle the situation presented?

- What if the homeowner doesn't agree with the final decision?

- What would the recourse for the homeowner be, if any?

- If the situation involves more than one homeowner, how does the board intend to handle the communication, so all parties are heard and points of view considered?

- At what point will be situation be finalized?

Rules of Conduct Policy

- Define the rules regarding noise.

- Define the rules regarding pets.

- Define the rules regarding parking.

- Define the rules regarding patio or deck use.

- Define the rules for what is and is not allowed in the common areas.

<u>Water Leak Policy</u>

- If a leak is strictly inside one unit, let the homeowner take care of it.

- If a leak affects more than one homeowner, a board member should initiate the resolution by calling a plumber, if need be.

- The board would pay the plumber with association funds. Then, invoice the homeowner whose pipe was responsible for the leak, if this is allowed in the governing documents. If it involves a pipe belonging to the building and to no one homeowner in particular, the association funds should cover the bill.

- For any damage caused by the water leak, if the damage is in the common areas, the board would take care of getting that area repaired. Whether or not a homeowner would be invoiced to reimburse the association for the damage would depend on the situation. If the damage is in a homeowner's unit, the homeowner would take care of getting that area repaired.

Monthly Dues Grid

2018	Jan.	Feb.	March	April	May	June	July	Aug.	Sept.	Oct.	Nov.	Dec.
1	√	√	√+	√								
2	√	√	√	√								
3	AW	AW	AW	AW	AW	AW	AW	AW	AW	AW	AW	AW
4	√	√	√	√								
5	√	√	√	√								
6	√	√	√	√								
7	√	√	√	√								
8	√	√	√	√								
9	AW	AW	AW	AW	AW	AW	AW	AW	AW	AW	AW	AW
10	AW	AW	AW	AW	AW	AW	AW	AW	AW	AW	AW	AW
11	AW	AW	AW	AW	AW	AW	AW	AW	AW	AW	AW	AW
12	√	√	√	√								
13	√	√	√	√								
14	√	√	√	√								
15	√	√	√	√								
16	√	√	√	√								
17	AW	AW	AW	AW	AW	AW	AW	AW	AW	AW	AW	AW
18	√	√+	√	√								
19	√	√	√	√								
20	√	√	√	√								
21	AW	AW	AW	AW	AW	AW	AW	AW	AW	AW	AW	AW
22	AW	AW	AW	AW	AW	AW	AW	AW	AW	AW	AW	AW
23	AW	AW	AW	AW	AW	AW	AW	AW	AW	AW	AW	AW
24	√	√	√	√								

1-24	unit numbers
AW	automatic withdrawal
√	dues paid
+	late fee applied

Typical Expenses

- carpet cleaning of the common areas
- dryer vent cleaning
- electricity
- fire extinguisher/smoke alarm inspection
- garbage & recyclables
- insurance
- lawn care/landscaping
- pest control
- management or accounting fees
- regular cleaning of common areas
- repair work: caulking, painting, etc.
- snowplowing
- tax filing
- water & sewer

Typical Maintenance Items

- caulking
- fixing dents, scratches, scrapes, broken pieces
- light bulbs
- painting

Board Meeting Notice

The next board meeting for the Any Name Association will be:

(Any date), at (any time) at (any location)

Condo owners don't have to attend but are welcome. We just ask that you let the board know if you plan to attend, so that if there are too many people, we can change the location to better accommodate everyone.

Board Meeting Agenda

(Any Association)
Board of Directors Meeting at (Any Location)
(Any Day), (Any Date)
(Any Time)

1. Call to order

2. Roll Call

3. Homeowner Input, if any

4. Financial Report; plus, dues status/invoices/checks.

5. Minutes of (any date) were approved via email.

6. Old Business:

    a. Carpet cleaning
    b. Caulking
    c. Tree trimming

7. New Business:

    d. Annual Meeting

8. Next board meeting date: (any date), (any day), (any time), at (any location).

9. Adjournment

Bare-Bones Board Meeting Minutes

Any Name Association Board Meeting
Any Day, Any Date, Any Time, Any Location

Present: (Board Members' Names)
Absent: (Board Members' Names)

The meeting was called to order at (any time).

Minutes. The board meeting minutes for (last date) were approved.

Financials. (Board member name) moved and (board member name) seconded to approve the (last month's) financials. The motion was passed by all.

Lawn Care. (Board member name) moved and (board member name) seconded to accept the renewal contract for XYZ Company. The motion was passed by all.

Caulking. (Board member name) moved and (board member name) seconded to have Company 123 caulk the patios of the main building. The motion was passed by all.

Next Meeting. The next condo board meeting will be held on (any day), (any date), (any time), (any location).

The meeting was adjourned at (any time).

- (Secretary's Name)
(Any association) Secretary

Expanded Board Meeting Minutes

Any Name Association Board Meeting
Any Day, Any Date, Any Time, Any Location

Present: (Board Members' Names)
Absent: (Board Members' Names)

The meeting was called to order at (any time).

Minutes. The board meeting minutes for (last date) were approved.

Financials. (Board member name) moved and (board member name) seconded to approve the (last month's) financials. The motion was passed by all.

Lawn Care. (Board member name) moved and (board member name) seconded to accept the renewal contract for XYZ Company. The motion was passed by all. The board chose to renew early and to lock in the price for a 3-year contract due to the great work the vendor has done for us.

Caulking. (Board member name) moved and (board member name) seconded to have Company 123 caulk the patios of the main building. The motion was passed by all. The board will also ask the contractor to check the caulking around the outside windows.

Next Meeting. The next condo board meeting will be held on (any day), (any date), (any time), (any location).

The meeting was adjourned at (any time).
- (Secretary's Name)
(Any association) Secretary

Appendices

Sample 2018 Budget

Account Description	YTD Total	1/31/18	2/28/18	3/31/18	4/30/18	5/31/18	6/30/18	7/31/18	8/31/18	9/30/18	10/31/18	11/30/18	12/31/18
Revenues:													
General Assessments	72,000.00	6,000.00	6,000.00	6,000.00	6,000.00	6,000.00	6,000.00	6,000.00	6,000.00	6,000.00	6,000.00	6,000.00	6,000.00
Interest	0.00	0.00	0.00	0.00	0.00	0.00	0.00	0.00	0.00	0.00	0.00	0.00	0.00
Sub-Total Revenues	72,000.00	6,000.00	6,000.00	6,000.00	6,000.00	6,000.00	6,000.00	6,000.00	6,000.00	6,000.00	6,000.00	6,000.00	6,000.00
Expenses:													
Accounting Services	4,200.00	350.00	350.00	350.00	350.00	350.00	350.00	350.00	350.00	350.00	350.00	350.00	350.00
Insurance/D&O/Property Cas.	12,000.00	1,000.00	1,000.00	1,000.00	1,000.00	1,000.00	1,000.00	1,000.00	1,000.00	1,000.00	1,000.00	1,000.00	1,000.00
Seasonal Services	4,980.00	415.00	415.00	415.00	415.00	415.00	415.00	415.00	415.00	415.00	415.00	415.00	415.00
Supplies	240.00	20.00	20.00	20.00	20.00	20.00	20.00	20.00	20.00	20.00	20.00	20.00	20.00
Electricity	1,440.00	120.00	120.00	120.00	120.00	120.00	120.00	120.00	120.00	120.00	120.00	120.00	120.00
Water/Sewer	144.00	12.00	12.00	12.00	12.00	12.00	12.00	12.00	12.00	12.00	12.00	12.00	12.00
Trash Removal	2,460.00	205.00	205.00	205.00	205.00	205.00	205.00	205.00	205.00	205.00	205.00	205.00	205.00
Tax Return/Audit	425.04	35.42	35.42	35.42	35.42	35.42	35.42	35.42	35.42	35.42	35.42	35.42	35.42
Carpet Cleaning	804.00	67.00	67.00	67.00	67.00	67.00	67.00	67.00	67.00	67.00	67.00	67.00	67.00
Structural Maintenance	12,865.00	1,500.00	1,500.00	1,500.00	1,500.00	1,500.00	1,500.00	1,500.00	1,500.00	1,500.00	1,500.00	1,500.00	1,500.00
Cleaning	3,384.00	282.00	282.00	282.00	282.00	282.00	282.00	282.00	282.00	282.00	282.00	282.00	282.00
Reserve	14,400.00	1,200.00	1,200.00	1,200.00	1,200.00	1,200.00	1,200.00	1,200.00	1,200.00	1,200.00	1,200.00	1,200.00	1,200.00
Sub-Total Expenses	57,342.04	5,206.42	5,206.42	5,206.42	5,206.42	5,206.42	5,206.42	5,206.42	5,206.42	5,206.42	5,206.42	5,206.42	5,206.42
Net Income	14,657.96	793.58	793.58	793.58	793.58	793.58	793.58	793.58	793.58	793.58	793.58	793.58	793.58

Sample Balance Sheet

ABC Association, Balance Sheet, February, 28, 2018		
ASSETS		
Current Assets		
Bank Checking Acct. #1	10,000	
Operating Savings Acct. #2	10,000	
Accounts Receivable	500	
Total Current Assets		**20,500**
Other Assets - Reserves		
Capital Reserve Savings Acct. #3	28,000	
Total Other Assets		**28,000**
Total Assets		**$48,500**
LIABILITIES AND CAPITAL		
Current Liabilities		
Accounts Payable	$3,500	
Prepaid Association Dues	3,500	
Total Current Liabilities		**7,000**
Long-Term Liabilities		
Total Long-Term Liabilities		**0**
Total Liabilities		**7,000**
Capital		
Retained Earnings	10,500	
Reserves Replacement	28,000	
Net Income	3,000	
Total Capital		**41,500**
Total Liabilities & Capital		**$48,500**
3/14/2018 - Unaudited - for Management Purposes Only		

Sample Income Statement

ABC Association, Income Statement, February 28, 2018						
	Current Month Actual	Current Month Budget	Current Month Variance	Year to Date Actual	Year to Date Budget	Year to Date Variance
Revenues						
General Assessments	$6,000	$6,000	0	$12,000	$12,000	0
Interest	10	0	10	15	0	15
Late Charges	30	0	30	45	0	45
Total Revenues	6,040	6,000	40	12,060	12,000	60
Expenses						
Accounting Services	350	350	0	700	700	0
Insurance	700	700	0	1,400	1,400	0
Seasonal Services	350	360	-10	750	720	30
Copies/Postage/Supplies	15	10	5	35	20	15
Electricity	150	125	25	300	250	50
Water/Sewer	0	200	-200	0	400	-400
Trash Removal	400	380	20	790	760	30
Legal	500	100	400	800	200	600
Tax Return/Audit	420	35	385	420	70	350
Structural Maintenance	260	100	160	0	200	-200
Cleaning	312	300	12	612	600	12
Fire & Safety	0	33	-33	0	66	-66
Grounds Maintenance	0	0	0	0	0	0
Reserves	1,208	1,000	208	2,416	2,000	416
Capital Expense	0	690	-690	0	1,380	-1,380
Total Expenses	4,665	4,383	282	8,223	8,766	-543
Net Income	$1,375	1,617	-242	3,837	3,234	603

For Management
Purposes Only

ABOUT THE AUTHOR

During an at-least 30-year span of condo living, Jewel has served on the board at various times. Currently, she has served as Vice President and Secretary since 2010.

Jewel is a business-to-business (B2B) copywriter and speaker specializing in the areas of personal and professional development/training. When not writing, speaking, or tending to condo board duties, she reads, works out, cooks, and studies foreign languages.

Should you have any questions or suggestions about the content in this book, you can email her at jewel@jewelpickert.com.

Notes

Notes

Notes

www.ingramcontent.com/pod-product-compliance
Lightning Source LLC
Chambersburg PA
CBHW070930270326
41927CB00011B/2794